Our Cat Flossie

For James, Rebecca and Sally Maidment

Our Cat Flossie

Ruth Brown

hinkler

Published by Hinkler Books Pty Ltd
45–55 Fairchild Street
Heatherton Victoria 3202 Australia
www.hinklerbooks.com

hinkler

First published by Andersen Press Ltd., London

Text © Ruth Brown 1986
Illustrations © Ruth Brown 1986
Cover design © Hinkler Books 2010

Cover design: Peter Tovey
Prepress: Graphic Print Group

ISBN: 978 1 7435 2441 1

Printed and bound in China

This is our cat Flossie.

She lives with us in London.

She likes the house and the garden, but does not
get on very well with the neighbours.

Her hobbies include birdwatching –

and fishing.

Flossie is a skilful climber

and an extremely enthusiastic gardener.

She always insists on helping with knitting

and making the beds.

She is very good at polishing shoes

but not quite so useful at Christmas-time.

**There are two things which she hates –
the sound of fireworks**

and visits to the vet.

Flossie loves collecting butterflies

and she is rather fond of snails

even though she finds them puzzling.

She is unable to resist a box

no matter what the size.

But, like all cats, most of all she loves to sleep…

and sleep…

and sleep.